The Blue Angels
FOR KIDS
by Eric Z

To all the kids who want to be a Blue Angels Pilot

If you persist, you will succeed!

Text and diagrams © 2016 Eric Z of www.TheKIDSBOOKS.BLOGSPOT.COM

All rights reserved

All other images cc-by-3.0:

 This file is a work of a sailor or employee of the U.S. Navy, taken or made as part of that person's official duties. As a work of the U.S. federal government, the image is in the public domain.

This file has been identified as being free of known restrictions under copyright law, including all related and neighboring rights.

Your FREE Gift

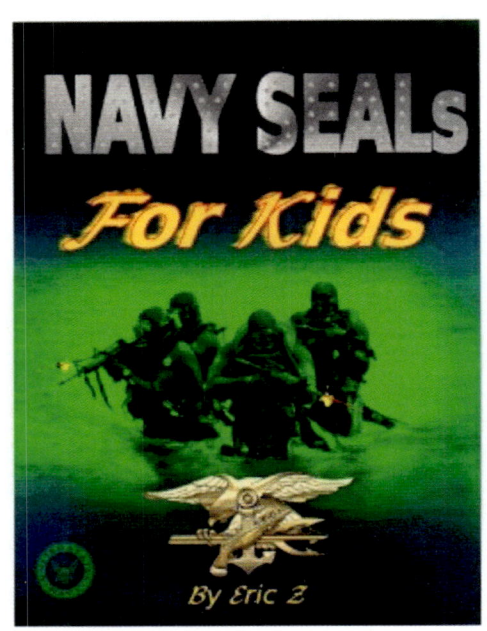

Navy SEALs for Kids

Obliterate the Leadership Gap!

Is at the END of this book

CONTENTS

Becoming a Blue Angel 7
Formations 9
   Delta Formation 9
   Diamond Formation 10
   Echelon Formation 11
Aerobatic Maneuvers 12
   Double Farvel 12
   Echelon Parade 13
   Fleur de Lis 14
   Fortus Maneuver 17
   Opposing Knife-Edge Pass 18
   High Performance Climb 21
   Aileron Roll 22
   Barrel Roll 23
   Diamond Roll 24
   Left Echelon Roll 25
   Diamond Loop 28
   Diamond 360 33
   Line Abreast Loop 34
   Low Break Cross 36
   Loop Break Cross (Delta Break) 38
   Sneak Pass 39
   Tuck Under Break 40
How do the Blue Angels make smoke? 41
McDonnell Douglas F/A-18 Hornet 43
     General characteristics 44
     Performance 44
G-suits 45
JATO / RATO 47
A History of the Blue Angels' Planes 48

"The mission of the Blue Angels is to showcase the pride and professionalism of the United States Navy and Marine Corps by inspiring a culture of excellence and service to country through flight demonstrations and community outreach."

For more information visit the official Blue Angels website: www.blueangels.navy.mil/show/

Becoming a Blue Angel

The Blue Angels pilots are chosen from the best Navy and Marines pilots. Each pilot must apply directly to the Blue Angels team, then the new pilots are selected by a VOTE by the current Blue Angels pilots!

If you want to become a Navy or Marine pilot, you must first become an OFFICER.

One of the best ways to become a Navy officer is to join the **Naval Reserve Officers Training Corps**, also called the Navy ROTC program. The Navy ROTC will even help pay for some of your college tuition!

www.nrotc.navy.mil

BUT...

No matter what age you are *now*, your path in the military,

as a Naval Aviator, also starts *NOW*.

You must strive to be the best person you can be. You must get the best grades in school, and above all you must **stay clean.**

"Stay clean" means don't get in trouble and never get arrested!

If you get arrested the military won't take you. After all, you will be flying the multi-million-dollar jets of the United States Navy: **You have to represent the best of the best.**

This book is about the Blue Angels, the bigger story about becoming a Navy Pilot is in this book "United States Navy Pilot"!

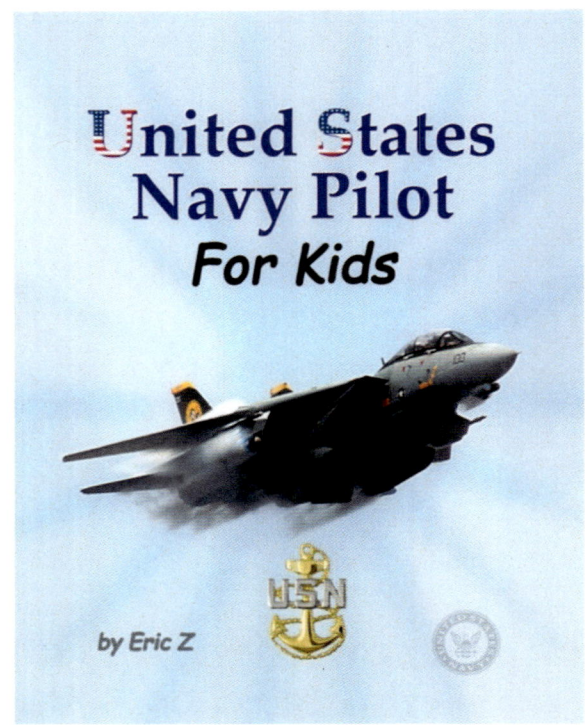

www.TheKidsBooks.Blogspot.com

Formations

The Blue Angels fly in 3 different formations.

Delta Formation

Diamond Formation

Front view of the diamond formation

Echelon Formation

Aerobatic Maneuvers

Double Farvel

In the double Farvel maneuver two aircraft fly upside down and two aircraft fly right side up. If only one aircraft flies upside-down it's called a single Farvel.

Echelon Parade

The Echelon parade is a simple maneuver in which the Blue Angels fly by in echelon formation.

Fleur de Lis

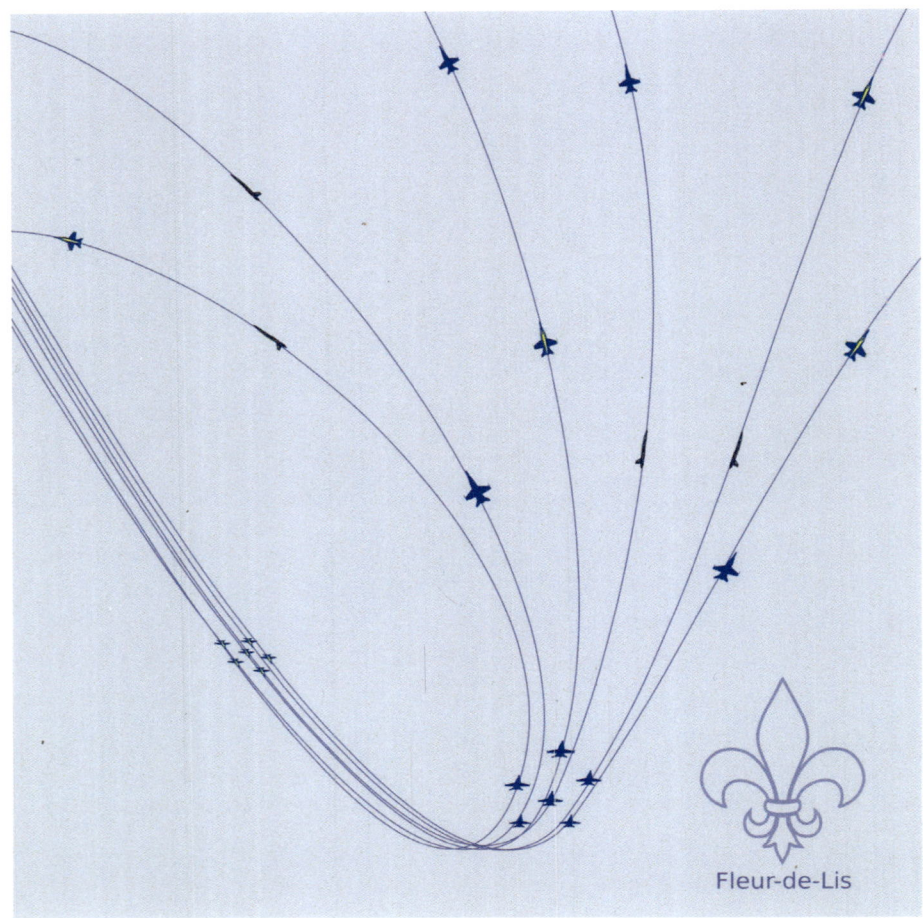

    This maneuver can be performed climbing, like in the picture above, or diving down at the ground!

    In this maneuver the blue angels fly in a five man formation kind of like the points of the Fleur-de-Lis. Then they break apart and fly in five different directions.

Watch the Blue Angels videos of these maneuvers here!

www.thekidsbooks.blogspot.com

Here we see an older picture of the Blue Angels performing the Fleur-De-Lis in the A4 Skyhawk downwards.

And here we see the Blue Angels in the newer F-18 performing the Fleur-De-Lis upwards.

Fortus Maneuver

In the Fortus maneuver one aircraft flies upside down and below the other, making a mirror effect. When done correctly it really looks like a mirror image of the other aircraft!

Opposing Knife-Edge Pass

    This is one of the scariest Maneuvers of the Blue Angels show. Two Blue Angels coming from different sides, fly at each other at high speed, and it looks just like they're going to crash into each other!

    From the ground this looks incredibly dangerous, and it is.

    But the Blue Angels fly within a couple yards between themselves and at the last second roll their aircraft on the side so they do not collide.

    This really shows you how professional and highly trained the Blue Angels pilots must be to perform such picture-perfect Air Shows.

High-Alpha Pass

This is sometimes called "tail sitting", the aircraft actually looks like it is sitting on its tail!

The "Section High Alpha" is the slowest maneuver of all.

During the maneuver the two jets slow down to 143 miles per hour as they pull the nose of the aircraft up to 45 degrees.

It's called "High Alpha" because the nose of the aircraft is so high and the "Angle of Attack" is also high. "Alpha" is just the short word for Angle of Attack. It is also abbreviated "A.O.A." .

Angle of attack is the angle of the aircraft ABOVE the horizontal, or horizon line.

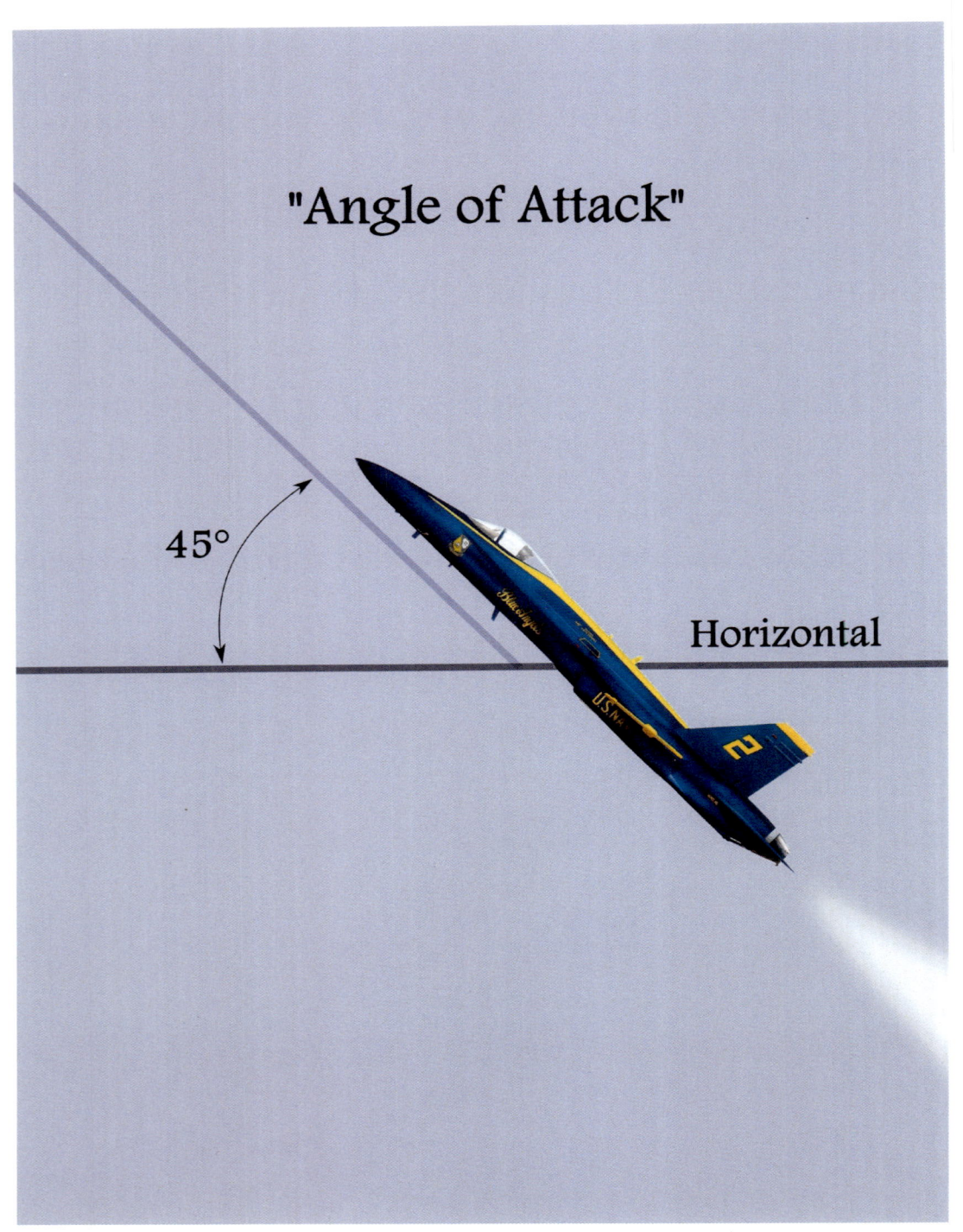

High Performance Climb

In the high performance climb one Blue Angel takes off from the ground and immediately pulls his aircraft up into a vertical climb at maximum thrust! It looks like the Blue Angel shoots right into the sky as his F-18 Hornet climbs quickly out of sight.

Aileron Roll

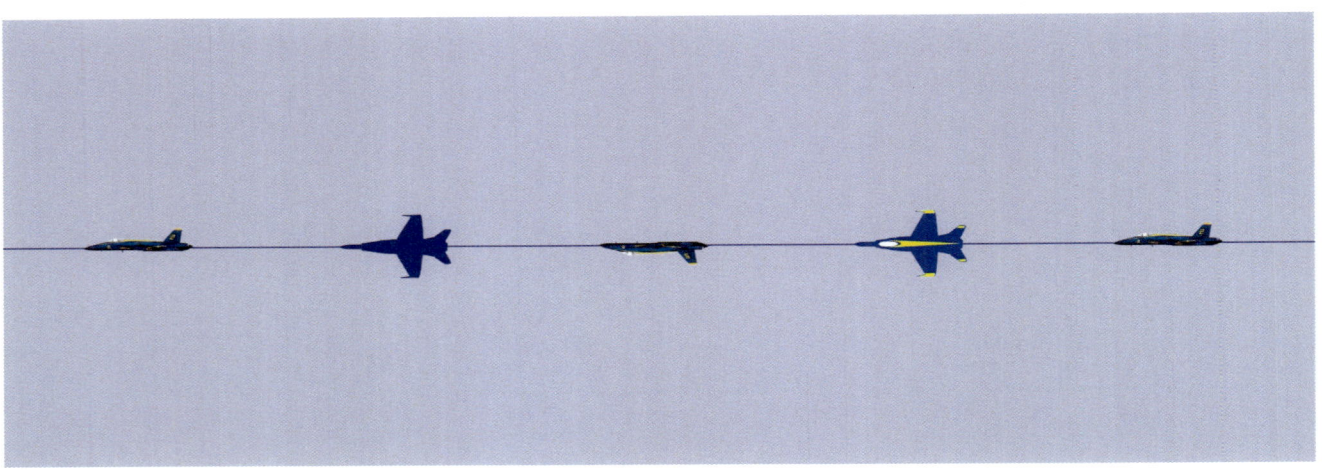

When an aircraft rolls perfectly around its nose, or "longitudinal axis", it is called an aileron roll. This is often confused with the "Barrel Roll" on the next page:

McDonnell Douglas F/A-18B Hornet

U.S. Naval Test Pilot School

Barrel Roll

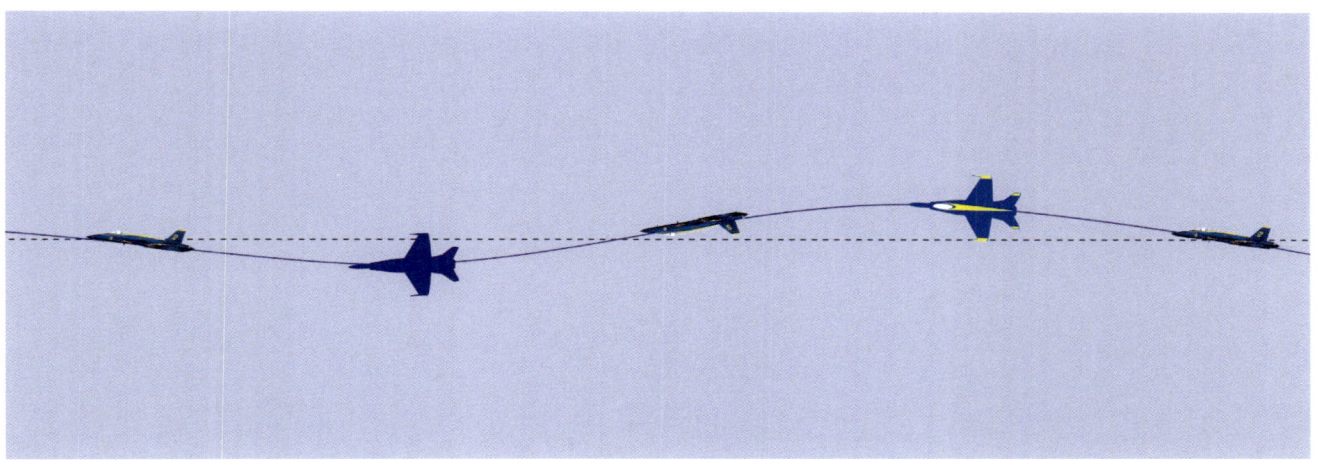

In the barrel roll, the aircraft does not fly a perfect horizontal line or path in the sky. Instead, the pilot pulls the nose up a little and the aircraft rolls like a barrel around the imaginary horizon line.

McDonnell Douglas F/A-18B Hornet

Diamond Roll

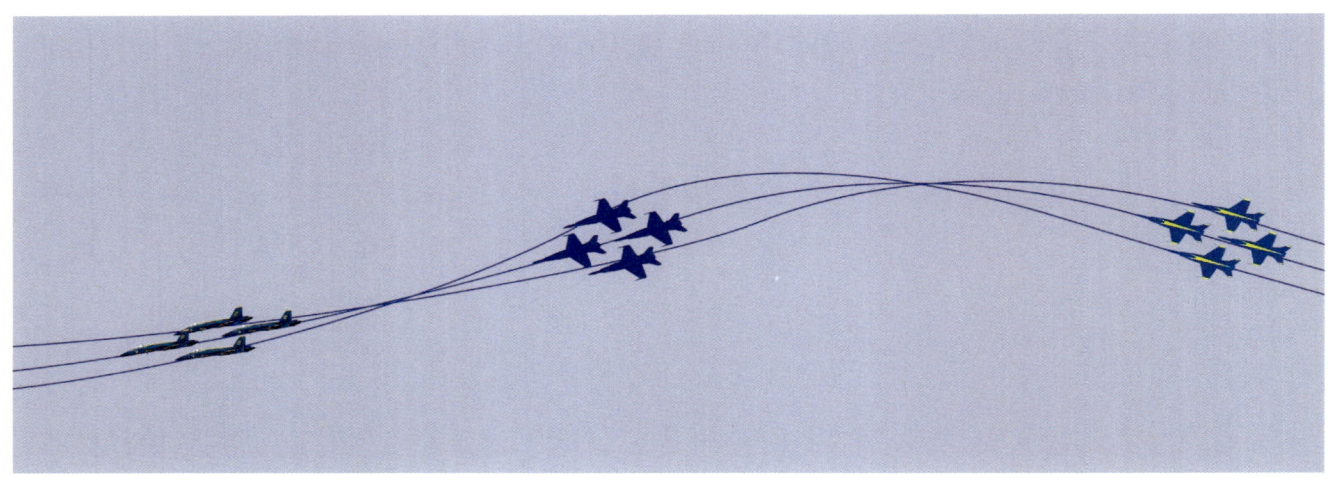

The Blue Angels fly in diamond formation and the entire formation performs a roll!

McDonnell Douglas F/A-18B Hornet

Disguised as an enemy aircraft for the Top Gun School

Left Echelon Roll

The Blue Angels fly in Echelon formation and perform a roll. The outside aircraft, that is the one all the way on the right of the formation, has a real challenge to keep up with the other aircraft!

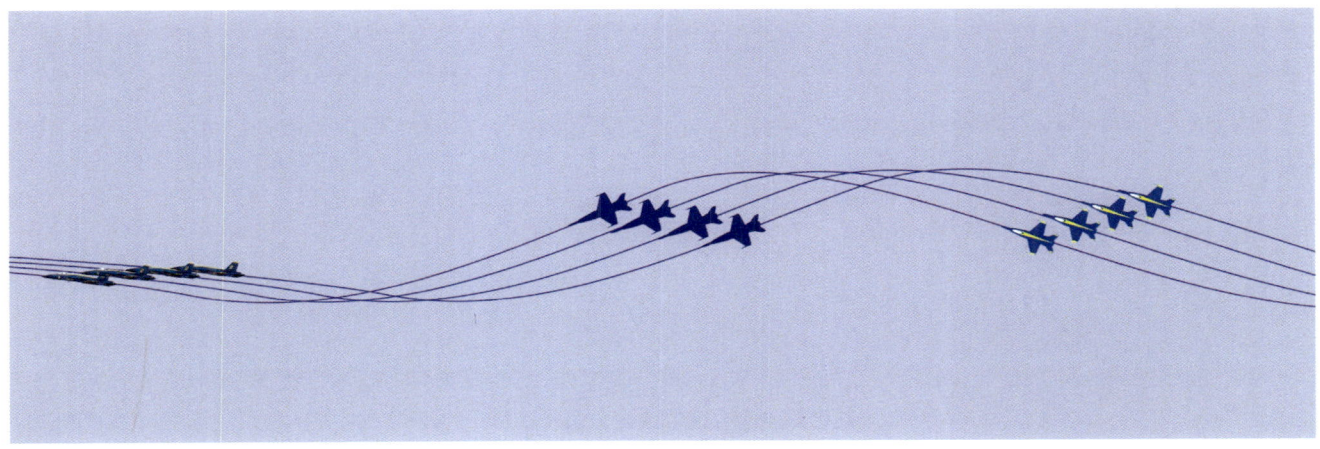

Watch the Blue Angels videos of these maneuvers here!

www.theKidsBooks.blogspot.com

Left Echelon Roll

McDonnell Douglas F/A-18A Hornet

Delta Roll

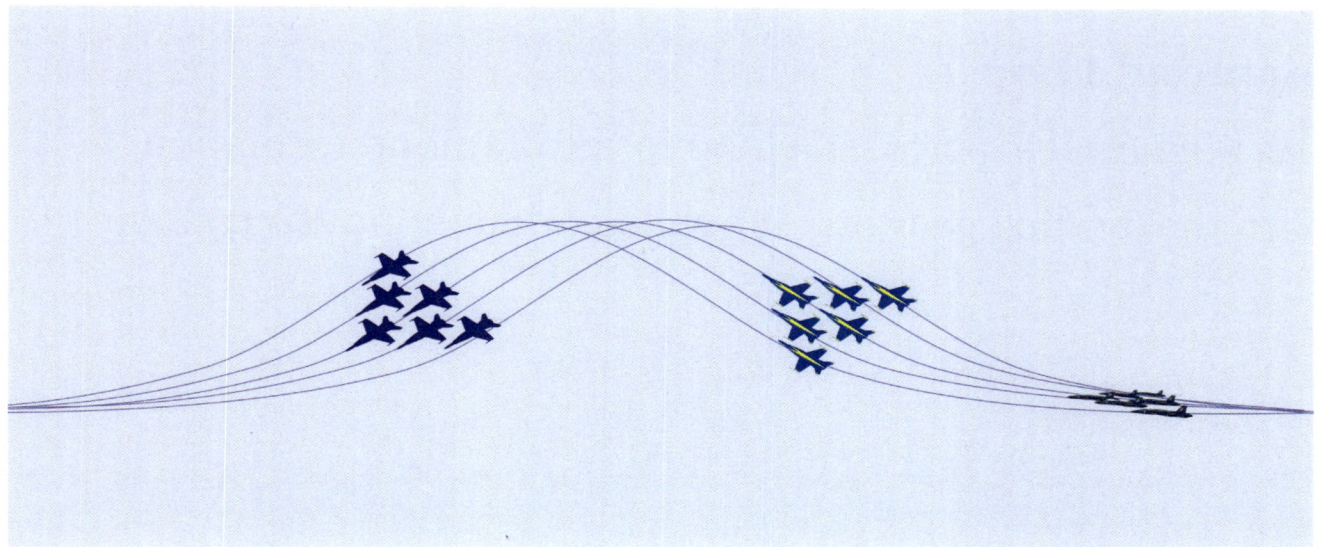

Another challenging maneuver: The Blue Angels fly in delta formation, and the entire formation performs a roll. This is easy for the planes in the middle, but the aircraft on the ends must really try to keep up with the others!

Diamond Loop

The Blue Angels perform a loop in the diamond formation. With the landing gear out, it's called a "diamond *dirty* loop"!

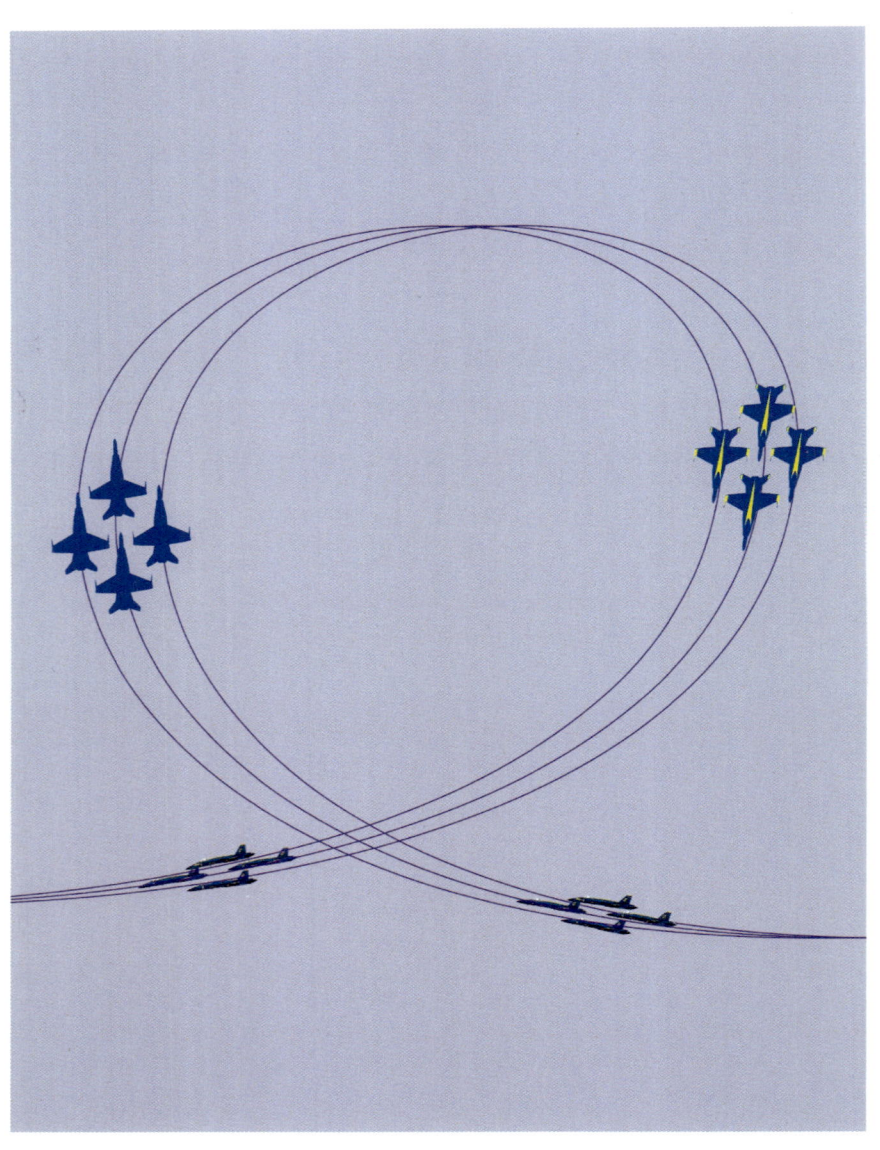

Diamond "Dirty" Loop

Diamond Loop

This is what it looks like for the pilot of the rear aircraft during the Diamond Dirty Loop!

Diamond Loop

Diamond 360

In the diamond 360 maneuver the Blue Angels fly a perfect circle around the Airfield in the diamond formation.

Line Abreast Loop

Line-Abreast Loop – the most difficult formation maneuver to do well. The Blue Angels have to keep their aircraft in a perfect line for the whole maneuver!

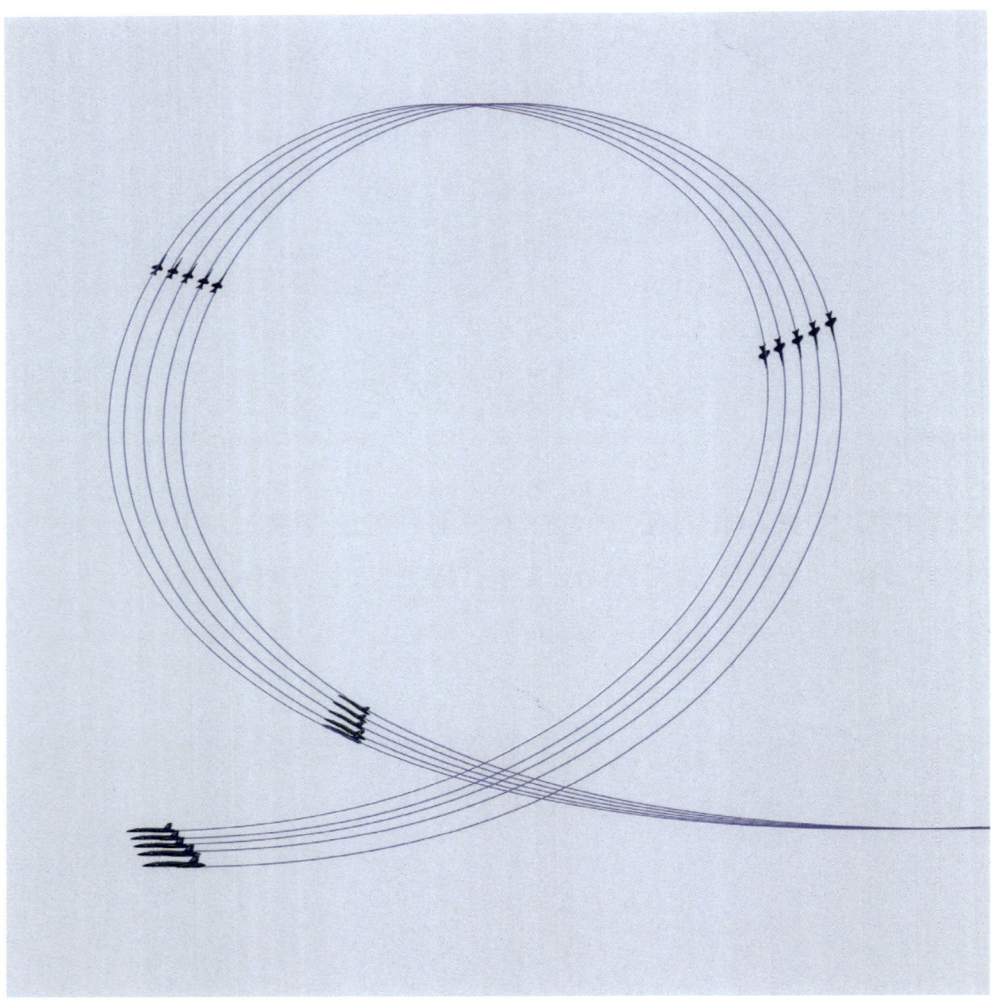

Line Abreast Loop

Low Break Cross

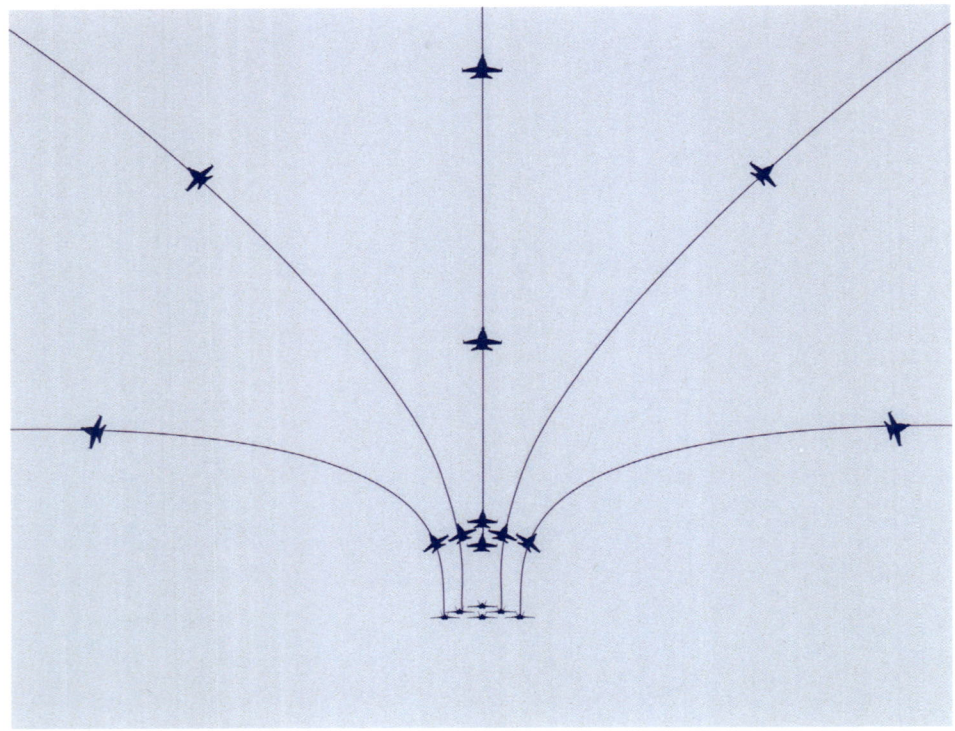

    This maneuver is especially spectacular when you are sitting right in the front middle of the showgrounds.

    The Blue Angels fly straight at you, and then at the last instant, "break" apart in all directions!

Low Break Cross

McDonnell Douglas F/A-18A Hornet

Loop Break Cross (Delta Break)

   In this maneuver the Blue Angels perform a loop in Delta formation. But when they are coming down from the loop and pointing right at the crowd from up above, they fly apart in all directions!

Sneak Pass

The sneak pass is another spectacular maneuver. One Blue Angel flies almost at the speed of sound, that's 700 miles per hour!

Not only that, but he flies very low, and because he's flying near the speed of sound you don't hear him coming. Suddenly right in front of you there's a Blue Angel flying by in a big blue blur! Then you hear the roar of the engines suddenly as the Blue Angel pilot takes off into the sky.

Tuck Under Break

In this maneuver the Blue Angels in echelon formation roll their aircraft one by one and leave the formation.

How do the Blue Angels make smoke?

The Blue Angels make smoke by pumping oil into the exhaust of their jet engines!

The Blue Angels F-18 Hornet aircraft do not have any guns, instead of the guns there is an oil tank.

In the picture below you can see the oil tube which goes into the left exhaust of the aircraft.

McDonnell Douglas F/A-18 Hornet

The Blue Angels fly a real combat aircraft, the McDonnell Douglas F-18 Hornet!

The aircraft have been modified, for example there is now a smoke generator in place of the machine gun. All of the Weapons Systems have been removed, and of course the battle gray paint has been changed to the nice Blue Angels color scheme.

Other changes have been made specifically for aerobatic maneuvers. But despite all of these changes, a blue angels aircraft could be quickly and easily repurposed back into military life as a lean mean combat fighting machine!

A Blue Angels F-18 Hornet on an Aircraft Carrier

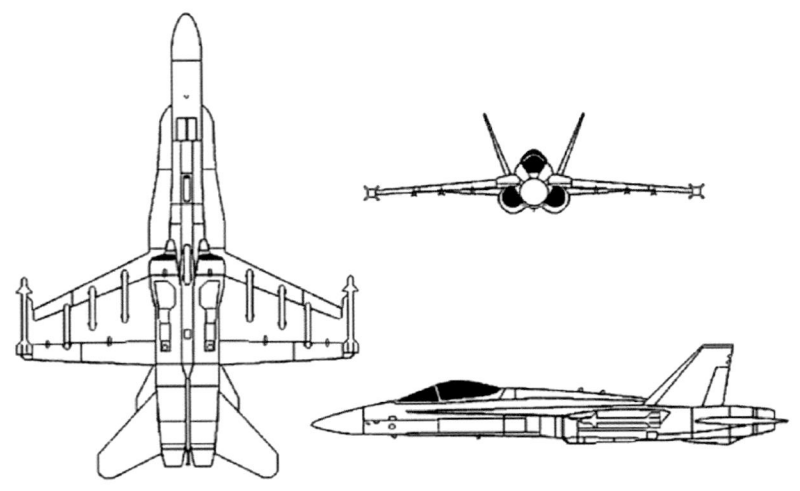

General characteristics

Length: 56 ft (17.1 m)
Wingspan: 40 ft (12.3 m)
Height: 15 ft 4 in (4.7 m)
Empty weight: 23,000 lb (10,400 kg)
Loaded weight: 36,970 lb (16,770 kg)
Powerplant: 2 × General Electric F404-GE-402 turbofans
Dry thrust: 11,000 lbf (48.9 kN) each
Thrust with afterburner: 17,750 lbf (79.2 kN) each
Fuel capacity: 10,860 pounds (4,930 kg) internally

Performance

Maximum speed:
High altitude: Mach 1.8 (1,034 knots, 1,190 mph, 1,915 km/h) at 40,000 ft (12,190 m)
Low altitude: Mach 1.2 (795 knots, 915 mph, 1,473 km/h)
Service ceiling: 50,000 ft (15,240 m)
Rate of climb: 50,000 ft/min (254 m/s)
Thrust/weight: 0.96

G-suits

The G-Suit is the dark green suit on top of his flight suit

All fighter pilots wear G-suits.

G-suits help the pilot stay CONSCIOUS during high-g maneuvers. "Hi G" is just a fancy word for very sharp curves, and turns, and loops.

Did you know that if you fly a loop, or turn the plane hard enough, the g-forces will push the blood in your body down towards your feet?

The blood in your body is not supposed to be in your feet, it's supposed to be in your head! — and when the blood leaves your head, you lose consciousness.

So the G-suit AUTOMATICALLY squeezes the legs and waist of the pilot during tight curves and loops. This keeps the pilot's blood in his upper body, and head, and keeps him conscious!

But the Blue Angels pilots don't wear G-suits.

Why not?

Because the Blue Angels fly so close to each other that they do not want to risk any UNCOMMANDED MOVEMENTS.

In the cockpit of an F-18 fighter jet, the control stick is very close to the knees of the pilot. During high G Maneuvers the G-suit might actually move the pilot's knees or legs accidentally, and hit the control stick. This could be very dangerous! Remember the Blue Angels pilots fly in formation just inches away from each other. Any uncommanded movement could cause a crash!

So how does a Blue Angels pilot stay conscious when he's doing very tight turns and loops all without a G-suit?

Blue Angels Pilots undergo more extensive training than a normal fighter pilot. The Blue Angels Pilots must tense their leg muscles to keep the blood in their head. This way they will not go unconscious during a high G maneuver.

JATO / RATO

One of the most spectacular parts of the Blue Angels show is when "Fat Albert", the Blue Angels transport aircraft takes off with its rockets!

This is known as JATO for "Jet Assisted Take Off" or RATO for "Rocket Assisted Take Off".

See the Fat Albert videos at TheKidsBooks.blogspot.com!

A History of the Blue Angels' Planes

Grumman F6F-5 Hellcat: June–August 1946

Grumman F8F-1 Bearcat: August 1946 – 1949

Grumman F9F-2 Panther: 1949 – June 1950 (first jet):

Grumman F9F-8 Cougar: Winter 1954/55 - mid-season 1957 (swept-wing)

Grumman F11F-1 (F-11) Tiger: mid-season 1957 – 1968 (first supersonic jet)

McDonnell Douglas F-4J Phantom II: 1969 – December 1974

Douglas A-4F Skyhawk: December 1974 – November 1986

McDonnell Douglas F/A-18A/B/C/D Hornet (F/A-18B/D are #7 aircraft): November 1986 – present

The End

I hope you enjoyed this book!

Join the KidsBooks and get your next book for FREE:

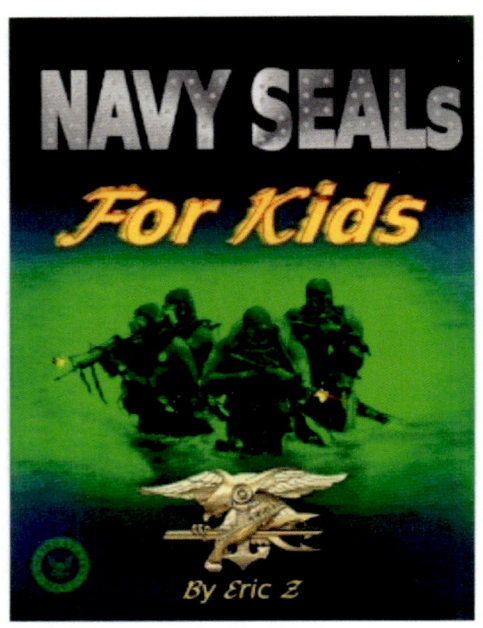

Navy SEALs for Kids

Obliterate the Leadership Gap!

Go to:

bit.ly/nvysls

Enjoy your free ebook!

(you have to type the link above EXACTLY in your browser!)

Made in the USA
Monee, IL
22 November 2019